silent birth

When Your Baby Dies

Sharon N. Covington, MSW, LCSW-C

Fairview Press
Minneapolis

Published by Fairview Press, 2450 Riverside Ave., Minneapolis, MN 55454. Fairview Press is a division of Fairview Health Services, a nonprofit, community-focused health system affiliated with the University of Minnesota, providing a complete range of services, from the prevention of illness and injury to care for the most complex medical conditions.

Library of Congress Cataloging-in-Publication Data
Covington, Sharon N.
  Silent birth : when your baby dies / Sharon N. Covington.
      p. cm.
  ISBN 1-57749-144-0 (saddle-stitch : alk. paper)
1. Stillbirth--Psychological aspects. 2.   Stillbirth--Popular works.
3.   Grief. I. Title.
  RG631.C686 2003
  618.3'2--dc21

2003011493

ISBN-13: 978-1-57749-144-6
Printed in the United States of America.

Editor: Deborah Rich, Ph.D.

Medical Disclaimer
This publication is designed to provide accurate and authoritative information in regard to the subject matter covered. If medical advice or other professional assistance is required, the services of a qualified and competent professional should be sought. Fairview Press is not responsible or liable, directly or indirectly, for any form of damages whatsoever resulting from the use (or misuse) of information contained in or implied by these documents.

Contents

Introduction

For many parents, pregnancy is a happy time. But when you have been told that your baby has died, everything changes. Prepared for birth, you are suddenly faced with death. Feelings of joy turn to grief. Instead of planning and hope, there is confusion and despair.

This booklet is based on the experiences of bereaved parents like you, many of whom were unprepared for their baby's death. Their frequent comment of "If only I had known" is the reason this booklet was written.

Silent Birth is for those couples who have lost a baby during pregnancy, labor, or shortly after birth. It may also help those who have learned during pregnancy that their baby has a terminal birth defect and that they must prepare for their baby's death. In addition, it can provide medical caregivers, family, and friends with an understanding of how to help bereaved families.

The booklet is intended for both parents, not just the mother. Sometimes when a baby dies, the father can feel pushed into the role of decision-maker and protector, and his own needs can be neglected. A baby's death is an experience that needs to be shared by both mother and father; both need the opportunity to grieve the loss.

This booklet will help you know what to expect and what to do when suddenly faced with the trauma of your baby's death. Your grief will heal better and faster if you can face your baby's death squarely rather than avoid it, postpone your response to it, or pretend your baby didn't exist. Though nothing will take your pain away immediately, it is hoped that this booklet will help you find a meaningful way to commemorate your baby's life, manage your grief, and lessen any later regrets.

Preparing for delivery

Delivery can seem like a cruel punishment if your baby has died during pregnancy or shortly after birth. At first you are in a state of shock. You need time to fully understand what is happening. If the diagnosis is made before you are admitted to the hospital and your labor has begun, it can be very helpful to have a day or two to plan for delivery, gather support, and prepare.

For the most part, the same principles you may have learned in childbirth class will apply to this delivery, as will your rights as a pregnant patient. But this delivery carries with it a different meaning. Therefore, you will feel the need to respond and act differently. Here are some things that other parents found to be comforting in their time of need. You may want to consider them to see what might be right for you.

Supportive people. During this emotional time, you will need extra support. Ask the hospital if there is a member of the staff with special knowledge of perinatal loss (a loss that occurs around the time of birth) who could be available to you throughout labor and delivery. This person, often a nurse or a social worker, can offer you direction, guidance, and understanding about perinatal loss, as well as inform you about hospital policy and your options. You may also want to have family members or close friends with you. Or you may decide that you want as much privacy as possible. Remember that, as in any birth, you can choose those you want around you. You should feel free to let the staff and your family and friends know what your needs are.

Creating mementoes. This is your child, and you may want to commemorate your child's life in a special way. Right now, it may not seem important to create remembrances and mementoes. But other parents have said how important these mementoes can be later on. When you go to the hospital, you may want to bring a camera for taking a picture of your baby, a special blanket or outfit that you can put on your baby, or small gifts for the baby, such as drawings or notes from family members.

Minimal medication. You may feel that you would like to be heavily medicated or put to sleep during delivery. However, the experience of other mothers has shown that using as little medication as possible and participating as fully in the birth as you had originally planned often facilitates grief. After delivery, you may want to avoid heavy sedatives. They can dull your awareness of this significant time, delay grieving, and hamper emotional healing.

Room assignment. Depending on hospital policy and room availability, you may be able to choose if you want to return to the obstetrical/gynecological (OB/GYN) unit. Do not feel afraid to go to the OB/GYN unit. These nurses often are the best at supporting your loss and grief. Since they know the joy a new baby can bring, they feel deeply the sadness and loss when a baby dies. You may also request a private room so that your partner can remain with you as much as possible, perhaps throughout the night. You can offer each other mutual support, and family members can visit more comfortably.

Saying goodbye

Your baby has become a person, known to you through your hopes, dreams, and imagination about him or her. It is natural to grieve the child and these thoughts. However, when you have little tangible evidence of your baby's existence, the grief process can become more difficult. For you and those close to you, there are some very real and meaningful ways that will help you say goodbye to your baby. They may also help you avoid later regrets.

Seeing your baby. Seeing, touching, and holding your baby may be the most important thing you can do. Although this may sound scary or morbid at first, many parents have found that seeing their baby helped them face their loss and begin the grieving process. Even if your baby has a physical abnormality, your fantasy about what the abnormality will look like is usually far worse than the reality. If you prefer, a blanket can be placed over the abnormality so that you are still able to see the perfect parts of your baby. Ask your doctor or nurse to help prepare you for this experience by explaining to you how the baby will look. You may want to have a staff person assist you. You should be given privacy and as much time as you want to rock, cuddle, look at, and talk to your baby. If you brought special clothes, you may want to dress the baby. If you brought a camera, you may want to take pictures of your baby clothed or undressed. Also, you may want to cut a lock of hair. Remember, while in the hospital, you can always ask to see your baby again. The staff should understand your difficulty in saying goodbye.

Mementoes. Ask the hospital for pictures of your baby, both clothed and undressed, being held by someone. If you don't want the pictures at first, request that they be placed in your medical record so that you may ask for them at a later time. The hospital may also be able to provide you with a cap, blanket, or comb and brush used by your baby; a special hospital certificate with your baby's feet and hand prints, along with a record of length and weight; wrist band; or any other item related to your baby. If your baby was issued a birth certificate and/or death certificate, you may later send for a copy from your local bureau of vital records. Some families create a special "memory box." This box can contain such things as the hospital mementoes, condolence cards, special gifts, personal notes, or a diary of your feelings about your baby and this experience.

Naming. Your baby is a person and deserves a name. You may want to use the name you planned or select another that has a special significance for this baby. Naming allows you to refer more easily to your baby in later conversations. It also helps others to understand that this baby was a real person to you.

Religious or cultural rituals. You may request that a clergy member, minister, or rabbi be available to perform a service and offer guidance. Or you may choose to do this yourself when you see your baby. If you have ethnic or religious customs that offer you and your family comfort, please let the hospital staff know. They will respect how you want to observe your customs or mourning rituals. The spiritual support person at the hospital should be able to assist you with any special arrangements.

Organ donation. If your baby was born alive late in pregnancy, it may be possible to donate certain organs. Some parents find comfort knowing that their baby has helped another child to live, and that a vital part of their baby lives on in another. If you are interested in pursuing this option, ask your health care provider if your baby can be a donor.

Autopsy or pathology report. Your doctor may ask permission to perform medical testing to try to determine the cause of your baby's death. Ask the doctor to explain to you what will happen to your baby at the autopsy, what information can be obtained, and what will be done with your baby afterwards. These reports can provide important information about why your baby died. However, some parents may never get a definite answer since much in this area is still unknown.

Burial or cremation. You will have to make a decision about what to do with your baby's body. If you would like to have a burial, the hospital can help you contact funeral homes. Many funeral homes charge parents only a minimal fee for a baby's funeral. If you want your baby cremated, similar arrangements can be made. Or the hospital may be able to assume responsibility for final disposition of your baby.

Funeral or memorial service. You may choose to have a religious or memorial service a few days, or even much later, after your baby's death. Allow enough time so that all family members can participate. This special service can include those people who have provided you with the greatest support. If you decide to have a funeral, you may want to consider having an open casket so that others may see and say goodbye to your baby. Some parents have a private funeral immediately and a larger memorial service a few months later. Or you may want to do something as simple and private as lighting a candle or planting a tree in your baby's memory.

Donations, flowers, or memorials. Before leaving the hospital, you may want to decide how you would like family and friends to express their sympathy. You may ask for donations to be made in your baby's memory to a perinatal loss support group, medical research foundation, charity, church, hospital, or other organization. If you don't want flowers at this time, ask the florist not to fill the orders. Request a credit and you can order the flowers at a later time. Or you may want to set up a memorial fund in your baby's name for a special project, program, or scholarship.

Returning home

It will be difficult to leave the hospital with empty arms and return home to a vacant nursery. You may have other children at home who need you. Family and friends will want to help but may not know how. Here are some suggestions to make this difficult transition easier.

Nursery. One of the first things you may want to decide is what to do with the baby's room and gifts. If you decide to put things away, it can be therapeutic for you to do this yourself, in your own time, rather than have someone do it for you before you return home from the hospital. Some parents decide to return gifts to the givers, and others want to keep them since they were never used. There is no protocol, no right or wrong. Your decision is very personal and should be what feels most comfortable to you.

Announcements. Some parents find it meaningful and helpful to write a short announcement about their baby's life and death to send to family and friends. Or you might ask a friend to take responsibility to let others know what happened and how they may express their sympathy to you. You may write a personal note to people or make an announcement card, such as the one below.

Anne and John Smith
sadly announce
the birth and death of their son
James Scott
March 8, 2007

In lieu of flowers
donations may be sent to
Fairview Pregnancy & Newborn Loss Center
2450 Riverside Avenue
Minneapolis, MN 55454

Memorial Service
April 19, 2007; 10:00 AM
Hospital Prayer Center
Fairview Riverside East
Minneapolis, Minnesota

You may receive many notes of condolence. People may not use the term "death" or "died" because it makes them uncomfortable. In fact, some people are so uncomfortable with the death of a baby that they may not write at all. However, below is what a note of condolence may sound like.

Dear Anne and John,

We were saddened to hear of the loss of your baby. We can only imagine the pain you must feel. Please know that we are with you in spirit as you mourn and that you have our deepest sympathy.

Love,
Susan and Bob

Each other. The death of a baby creates a crisis in any marriage. It can bring couples closer together or push them farther apart. You can help each other by openly sharing your feelings while accepting that you may have different emotions and may experience them at different times. Just as each of you has bonded in your own way with the baby, each of you will grieve in your own way. This is a difficult and fragile time. When you are hurting, you may not be able to give and receive support as you have at other times. It can be difficult to resume love-making since it can remind you of your baby. Still, you should try to allow yourself this special shared pleasure. Be patient with each other, and keep communication open.

Your other children. If you have other children, it is important not to shield them from what is going on or from the pain you are feeling. Recognize, understand, and share their pain. Let them know that you feel the same way. This is an opportunity to bond with your children in a special way. Give them simple and honest explanations about what has happened, keeping in mind their age and ability to understand. Reassure them that there was nothing they did to cause the baby's death.

Realize that your other children, like you, will be grieving for a long time. Children have more difficulty than adults identifying their feelings. They may express them in many different ways: angry, argumentative, or oppositional behavior; nightmares, bed wetting, or other sleeping problems; difficulty separating from you; crying or whining; or other regressive behaviors. These behaviors don't usually last long, but your children may need continued help putting their feelings into words. If problems persist, consult your pediatrician. You may also consider professional counseling to assist your family through this difficult time.

Other people. You may find that at first you receive a great deal of support from other people. With time, however, this support may diminish. Some people will expect you to have recovered from your baby's death in just a few weeks. This expectation may come at a time when your pain is the greatest. Others may want to help but don't know how. You will need to tell people what you want from them and how you are feeling. For example, even though you may want to talk about your experience, people around you may be afraid to bring up the subject. Or they may make inappropriate or hurtful comments, such as "You can always have another baby," or "At least you didn't know the baby." Even though people aren't intentionally thoughtless, you should put your needs first. You don't have to be polite or brave for other people.

Your job. If you had planned to take a leave of absence from your job after your baby was born, you should take it now anyway. It is important not to rush back to work as if nothing has happened. Now is not the time to hurriedly "put things back the way they were" or resume a heavy workload. You have had a child, and your child has died. This is a significant time in the life of a family and should be respected as such. Returning to the pressures of your job and seeing your co-workers can be hard. Wait until you are feeling stronger physically and emotionally before taking on this formidable task.

You might want to inquire about your company's policy on funeral and death leave. Many companies provide special leave for a death in the immediate family, which is what your baby's death was. This time could be used instead of or in addition to your planned use of maternity and annual leave.

Feeling the Loss

Grieving is the emotional response to a loss. Mourning is the way we deal with these emotions. Parents in mourning usually suffer some or all of the following feelings, although in no particular order or length of time.

Shock and numbness. A feeling of disbelief and the sense that this can't really be happening can last for a few hours or a few weeks. It is not uncommon for these feelings to come and go in waves for the first few months.

Yearning and searching. You may experience intense feelings of anger, sadness, and guilt as you try to understand why this has happened. Anger may be directed towards those closest to you (spouse, family, friends) or those seen as having power and control over you (doctor, God). When the anger is directed inward, it becomes depression. Guilt can be overwhelming. In trying to find the answer, you often blame yourself. ("It must have been something I did or didn't do," or "I am being punished.") These feelings can make you wonder if something is wrong with how you are handling the loss.

Loneliness and depression. As intense emotions start to fade, the reality of your loss sets in along with feelings of sadness, fatigue, and powerlessness. These feelings may peak between three and nine months following your baby's death.

Acceptance and resolution. Early on, it may seem impossible that you will ever be able to accept what has happened to you. Yet, over time, the painful feelings become less frequent and intense. Your baby's death has become a part of your life experience—not in the sense of being right or fair, but simply as a fact of life. For many couples, the healing process takes from one to two years.

Shadow grief. Feelings of sadness often are rekindled around significant days or events, such as the date of conception, due date, birth date, or anniversary of the baby's death. Holidays like Mother's Day and Father's Day can also be painful. Changes of season or special places may trigger sad memories of your baby. However, the sadness will be a dull ache, not the encompassing pain it was at first. Many parents worry that once they resolve their grief they will forget their baby. Shadow grief serves as a reminder that your baby will always be in your heart.

Physical pain. Your grief may be expressed physically. Symptoms may include difficulty healing from the delivery, headaches, muscle spasms, susceptibility to infections, colds, and other viruses, aching breasts and arms, difficulty sleeping, lack of appetite, heart palpitations, shortness of breath, difficulty concentrating, forgetfulness, or tiredness. Sometimes grieving mothers feel as if their bodies have failed them. Tell your doctor of any concerns you have about your physical or emotional healing.

Time to heal

Grieving is hard work that takes time and drains energy. Be aware that your reactions are normal, with many ups and downs. Grieving takes far longer than society recognizes. In fact, integrating the death of a baby is a life-long process. Give yourself time to allow this complex process to occur. Here are some ways to help yourself cope.

Books. There are many books on perinatal loss that can offer knowledge, guidance, and support. These books can provide you with a greater understanding of your grief, how the death of a baby affects your life, and ways to cope.

Support groups. The most important factor in recovering from loss is having strong support. Even if you are receiving support from your family and friends and from your spiritual or faith community, you may find it helpful to join a community support group. A support group is usually made up of parents helping other grieving parents. Although individual experiences may vary, being with those who share the common bond of having lost a baby can be very comforting. Your healing will be helped by learning from the experiences of others. There are also reliable national organizations that offer support and resources, including Bereavement Services, RTS (800-362-9567 ext. 54747; www.bereavementprograms.com), Grief Watch (503-284-7426; www.griefwatch.com), National Share Office (800-821-6819; www.nationalshareoffice.com), and the Center for Loss in Multiple Births, Inc. (907-222-5321; www.climb-support.org).

Counseling. If you have become stuck in the grief process or can find little joy in life, you may want to seek professional help. The death of a baby can rekindle many hurts from the past. These rekindled hurts can complicate the healing process.

If this was already a difficult time in your life, before or during your pregnancy, grieving may be even more painful. For example, a recent move, stress at work, infertility history, or problems in a relationship can make the loss of a baby even more hurtful. Counseling can help you get through this difficult time. Ask your doctor, nurse, hospital social worker, or support group for names of therapists who have special skills in perinatal loss counseling.

Considering another pregnancy. Often couples will feel an urgency to become pregnant again as soon as possible, thinking that this will fill the emptiness and take the pain away. But grieving a baby's death is a difficult task, and becoming pregnant too quickly may complicate and short-circuit the grieving process. Realize that for a year following your baby's death you will be reliving memories of the pregnancy. Therefore, allow yourself sufficient time to heal both physically and emotionally before attempting another pregnancy.

Anticipating difficult times. Anniversaries of your baby's death, holidays, and due dates can be especially difficult times. Days that others may seem to have forgotten the significance of, you may be anticipating with sadness and dread. Let others know how you are feeling so that when the day arrives, you are not left doubly disappointed. Parents have found it helpful to plan something meaningful on special days, such as a dinner or religious service. Or you may want to do something in your baby's memory, such as make a donation, light a candle, or create a special ritual. Anticipating these painful times, letting others know what you are feeling, and finding a meaningful way to commemorate your baby will help you heal.

Grief is an ongoing process. Time really will help you come to terms with your baby's death. Reaching out to others will also help you cope with this tragic event. Perhaps one day the grief you feel now will enable you to help someone else who has suffered a similar loss.

Resources

Fairview Health Services. *Holiday Hope: Remembering Loved Ones During Special Times of the Year.*

Faldet, Rachel, and Karen Fitton, eds. *Cuando el embarazo termina en pérdida: nuestras historias.* (Spanish-language edition of *Our Stories of Miscarriage: Healing with Words.*)

Freda, Margaret Comerford, and Carrie Ann Semelsberger. *Miscarriage after Infertility: A Woman's Guide to Coping.*

Levang, Elizabeth. *The Remembering with Love Journal: A Companion for the First Year of Grieving and Beyond.*

Levang, Elizabeth. *When Men Grieve: Why Men Grieve Differently and How You Can Help.*

Levang, Elizabeth, and Sherokee Ilse. *Remembering with Love: Messages of Hope for the First Year of Grieving and Beyond.*

Fairview Press publishes books and related materials that educate individuals and families about their physical, emotional, and spiritual health and motivate them to seek positive changes in themselves and their communities. To receive a free catalog or to order Fairview Press titles, call (toll-free) 800-544-8207 or visit our Web site at www.fairviewpress.org. Organizations are encouraged to contact Fairview Press for information on discounts and customization.